Making
Friends

© Aladdin Books Ltd 2008

Designed and produced by
Aladdin Books Ltd

First published in 2008
in the United States by
Stargazer Books
c/o The Creative Company
123 South Broad Street
Mankato, Minnesota 56002

Illustrator: Christopher O'Neill

The author, Sarah Levete, has written and edited many books for young people on social issues and other topics.

Printed in the United States

Library of Congress Cataloging-in-Publication Data

Levete, Sarah.
  Making friends / by Sarah Levete.
      p. cm. -- (Thoughts and feelings)
  Includes index.
  ISBN 978-1-59604-152-3 (alk. paper)
  1. Friendship--Juvenile literature. 2. Loneliness--Juvenile literature. I. Title.

BF575.F66L48 2007
158.2'5--dc22
                        2007009187

Making Friends

Sarah Levete

Stargazer Books

Contents

Introduction

It's good to have friends. Friends can have fun together and trust each other. Sometimes it's nice to be by yourself. At other times if you are alone but want to be with other people, you may feel lonely. The children in this book will share with you their ideas on making friends and the ups and downs of friendships.

Feeling Lonely

Amy and Sacha have gone to the park. Amy is telling Sacha that sometimes she feels lonely because she has just moved to the area and doesn't know many people. There are lots of reasons why a person may feel lonely. Have you ever felt lonely?

It can be great to be alone... but it can also be lonely.

I miss my friends from my old school. Do you ever feel lonely?

Sometimes, but often I like to be by myself.

▶ It's OK To Be Alone

Being alone does not mean you are lonely. It can be fun to watch a TV program or read a book all by yourself. But at other times, if you want to chat to a friend and there is nobody there, then you may feel lonely.

◀ Do They Like Me?

Sometimes it can seem as if everybody else has lots of friends, except for you. That can make you feel lonely, and a bit jealous too. Feeling lonely can also make you nervous about making friends.

▶ The Same, But Different!

From our heads down to our toes, we are all different. But whether you are big or small, or whether your skin is black or white, we are all people who deserve friendship and respect. It can feel lonely if a person is unkind or leaves you out because you are different. People who do this miss out on some good friendships.

I wish I had some friends to play this with.

Story: Liam Gets Angry

1 Liam's dad gave him a game for his birthday. But he had no one to play with.

2 Liam hoped his new game would help him to make friends at school.

Don't you want to play my game?

No. We've got another game.

Nobody wanted to play that game. I hate you!

3 Liam shouted at his dad because the game hadn't made him any new friends.

Why was Liam mad at his dad?

Liam felt lonely and angry. He took his feelings out on his dad. That wasn't very fair. It wasn't his dad's fault that Liam found it difficult to make friends. Feeling lonely can make you grumpy and angry with the people who care about you. It would have made Liam feel better if he had told his dad how he felt.

This will teach them not to ignore me.

▶ I Don't Care . . .

Sometimes feeling lonely can make you feel mean. You may think that there is no point in being nice to others because you will never have any friends anyhow. But being mean to others will only make you feel more lonely and more unhappy.

Why don't you want to go to school?

◀ I'm Scared

Feeling lonely can make you lose confidence in yourself. You may not want to go to school because being with lots of other people can make you feel even more alone. Sometimes if somebody does try to make friends with you, you may feel too unsure to be friendly back.

▶ Just Me And My Computer...

Some people who find it hard to make friends hide in their bedroom and spend hours playing on their computer. But it's also good to get out and meet real people!

Amy, what did it mean to you to feel lonely?

"I felt as if nobody would ever like me. I thought I would never have anybody to play with. When we moved here, I missed my old friends. Everybody else at my new school already knew each other, and they all seemed to have friends. It made me mad at my mom for making us move here. After a bit, I began to feel more at home and became good friends with Sacha."

Friends Are Important

Josh and Marcus are talking about why friends are important to them. Marcus enjoys having lots of friends because he can do different things with them. Josh likes being able to tell his friends jokes, even if they don't laugh at them!
Why are friends important to you?

Friends make some things easier!

I like playing football with some friends and watching movies with others.

I can tell friends things that I can't tell other people.

▶ Good Times

Have you ever been told a really funny joke and wanted to tell someone else, to make them laugh? You can share good times with friends. You can laugh with friends, even if they tell rotten jokes!

I've been dying to tell you this all day.

◀ Bad Times

If you've had a difficult day at school or argued with your mom, dad, or carer, it can really help to talk things over with a friend. A friend can't make a bad day go away, but it certainly helps to be able to talk.

▶ Homework Buddy

Friends can help you in lots of other ways, like explaining difficult problems, or helping you with your homework. Sometimes a brother or sister can be a very good friend and help you in this way.

I've never been able to do this.

Don't worry, I'll help you.

Yasmin, what do friends mean to you?
"I have a few good friends who matter to me very much. We laugh and can tell each other how we feel. You can talk to friends when you're angry and know that they will understand. Friends are people you trust and who make you feel safe and happy. Mom and Dad are my friends, too."

Making Friends

Grace has made some good friends in her new school, even though it took her a long time to believe anyone would like her. There are lots of different ways to make friends but it's important to remember that friends are people you can trust. People who make you feel uncomfortable are not friends. If you feel unsure about someone, tell a grown-up.

Making friends can be easy.

Would you like to join in our game?

I was too scared to talk to you at first.

I thought you didn't like me because you never talked to me.

▶ Who Will Notice Me?

Sometimes, it may seem as if everybody else is always saying something funny or smart or has better games to play. Don't worry—everybody can feel like that sometimes. In fact, everybody else probably feels the same as you.

◀ Sing And Dance

Have you ever thought of joining a club or a group? It's a great way to meet people. You may feel shy at first, but you won't be the only one. Making friends can be fun—why not make a song and dance about it?

▶ Silent Friends

Cats and dogs can be good friends. So can an imaginary friend that no one else can see. But it's also important to have "real" friends of your own age, who you can chat to, and have fun with. "Real" friends can cheer you up too.

15

Be my friend, and I'll buy you some candy.

▶ Does It Feel Ok?

Nobody should offer you presents to become friends. People who make threats aren't really friends, either. If a person does this or makes you feel uneasy or says your friendship must be a secret, tell a grown-up you trust.

◀ Help Make It Easy

If you see someone who looks a bit lost and alone, why not ask him or her to join in with your friends? It may not make much difference to you, but it may make someone else feel happy.

Grace, do you make friends easily?

"Not really. Sometimes I think that nobody will like me—that makes me feel shy. Though I don't always feel like it, I make an extra effort to be friendly at school. It makes it easier when other people make an effort to include me too. Jan asked me to play and now we're good friends. But I wouldn't make friends if a person made threats; I would tell my mom."

They've noticed me, so why aren't they my friends?

Story: Finding a Friend

1 Jo wanted to make friends. She tried pushing in, but the others ignored her.

They ate my candy, then walked away!

2 Jo gave her candy away to try and make friends. It didn't work.

I'd love to play. Thanks for asking!

3 Jo asked Susie to play. Susie said yes. Jo and Susie soon became friends.

Why did Jo find it hard to make friends?

There is no magic recipe for making friends. Sometimes, it can be easy but at other times it can seem very hard. As Jo discovered, pushing in doesn't work—it's not very friendly. "Buying" friends doesn't work, either. What happens if you run out of candy? The best way to make friends is to be friendly, and to be yourself!

Different Friendships

Kelly is reading Amy a really funny bit from an email from her friend Ben who lives far away. Kelly doesn't see Ben very often but they write to each other. There are lots of different types of friendships, from best friends to gangs of friends. Can you think of any other types of friendships?

Try writing to a friend.

Brilliant! Ben's coming to visit me.

He sounds really nice.

▶ Who Is Your Friend?

You may be surprised to realize that your mom, dad, carer, brother, or sister is actually good fun as a friend, too. There are no rules about who you can be friends with, as long as they make you feel good and comfortable.

◀ Best Friends

Some people have several friends, but one BEST friend. This is often the friend to whom a person feels closest. It's great having a best friend, but don't worry if you don't have one. All types of friends are equally important.

▶ Vacation Friends

Everyone likes to have old friends who understand them. But it can also be fun to make new friends, even if it's just for a few days. It can be easy to make friends when you are on vacation, even though you may not see them after you go home.

Jimmy, can you tell us about your different friends?

"My best friend is Sam. We tell each other everything but I'm not telling you what! However, I have lots of different friends. My sister is a good friend, even though I get mad at her when she beats me at soccer. Sometimes I go around in a gang with lots of friends—that's fun, too."

Difficult Times

Dylan is telling his sister that he is mad at his best friend, Gavin, because Gavin went off to play soccer with someone else. Sometimes, even best friends like Dylan and Gavin have arguments. Being friends with a person is not always easy. Can you think of reasons why being friends can be difficult?

Arguments don't last forever.

It's not fair. Gavin should have asked me to play.

But maybe he wanted to play with someone else?

It's not fair. He gets everything he wants.

◀ **Feeling Jealous**

You may feel jealous of a friend because he or she has a game that you want, or has been invited to a party instead of you. But part of being a friend is enjoying someone else's good luck, however difficult that is!

▶ **Don't Worry!**

If you have ever been left out of a game or not been invited to someone's party, you will know that it can make you feel really grumpy and lonely. Remember, it happens to everyone. It doesn't mean that nobody likes you or you will never be included.

Why hasn't anyone chosen me?

Why doesn't he like me any more?

◀ **What's Gone Wrong?**

It can be upsetting when someone you like or are close to, suddenly doesn't want to be your friend. You may not understand why. But friendships do change over time and we all have to accept that, although it is hard.

22

Story: Anita Gets Jealous

1 Penny and Anita were best friends. They walked to school together.

Hi, Molly. Why don't you walk with us?

Hi, Penny.

2 One day, they met another friend of Penny's, called Molly. Anita looked angry.

Go away, Molly. Penny's my friend!

3 Anita didn't want Penny to have other friends.

Why was Anita angry?

Anita didn't think that Penny could be friends with both her and Molly. Anita might have liked Molly if she had given her a chance. Sometimes you may feel jealous of the other friends that a person has. But just because a person has more than one friend, it doesn't mean that they like you any less, or that you are any less special to them.

I dare you to take that comic!

▶ Say "NO!"

If a so-called friend dares you to do something that you feel is wrong, don't do it, even if he or she makes fun of you. So-called friends like that aren't worth it. It is better to lose a friend than to do something you know is wrong.

You're my best friend, Megan, but what you did was wrong.

◀ Say Something

Nobody has the right to hurt someone else or make anyone feel unhappy. If you see a friend being unkind to someone, explain why you feel what they did was wrong. Friends can be wrong sometimes!

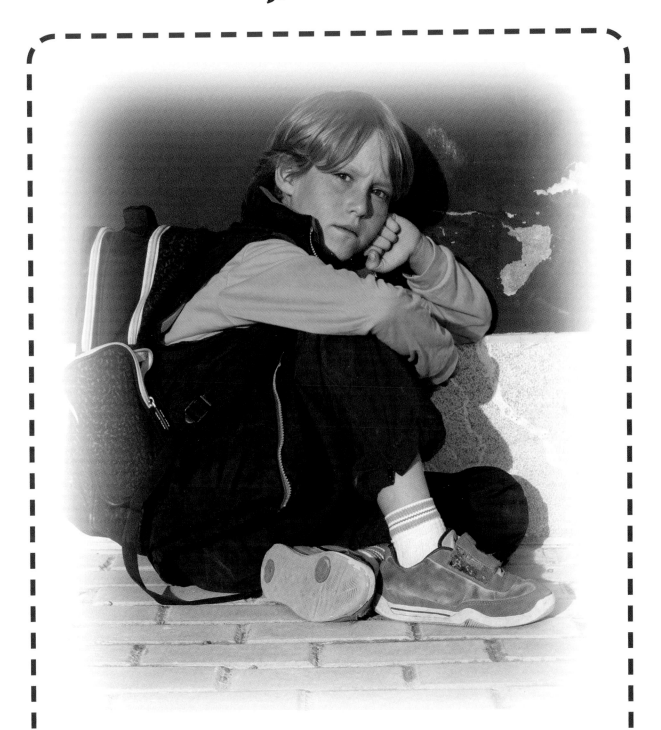

Alex, have you had problems with friends?

"I hung around with a gang who started stealing. They told me to keep it a secret, but I didn't want to join in. I talked to my dad and decided to leave the gang. I'm glad I did. Secrets are great, but there are some secrets that good friends wouldn't ask you to keep. If it feels wrong, say NO."

Working At Friendships

Megan and Nicole are at Charlotte's sleepover party. They have made up— they are best friends again! Megan and Nicole know that friends can have good and bad times. Telling a friend how you feel can help keep a friendship friendly. Can you think of other ways to work at friendships?

Mad at someone?
Why not talk instead?

I'm sorry about what happened. I'm glad we sorted it out.

Me too. I felt so much better after we had a talk.

She's great, isn't she!

▼ Try Talking!

If you and a friend have an argument or get mad at each other, tell each other how you feel. If you still feel mad, why not ask your mom or dad to sit with you both so you can sort it out?

I think I understand.

▲ Make Space!

It's important to think about other people's feelings. Sometimes you may be the center of attention, but at other times you won't. Try to remember that there's lots of time for everyone.

Megan, what are your tips for staying good friends?
"I think that the most important thing is to tell a friend how you feel even if you're really angry with them. Unless you can say sorry and forgive each other, you might stay mad forever. Friends are special, so try not to lose them!"

Don't Forget...

1

What does a good friend mean to you, Jimmy?

"It means having someone you can talk to, even if you are sad or angry. You can have a joke with a friend. But sometimes you have to say you're sorry, like I did with Sammy. But because he's my friend, he didn't stay mad at me—we even joked about it later."

2

How do you feel about making friends, Yasmin?

"I still feel a bit nervous about making friends, but I try to make an effort to be friendly. My mom persuaded me to try out for the school play. I met some really nice people there. I think we were all nervous, but once we got talking it was fun. I got a part, too!"

3

Is there a difference between being alone and feeling lonely, Amy?

"Yes. When you are by yourself and feel good about it, that's not feeling lonely. Feeling lonely is when you want to be with a friend, but there is nobody there. I felt lonely when we moved house. I really missed my old friends. It was difficult until I made some new friends."

4

Can you make sure no one feels lonely, Megan?

"Not really, but you can try to make everyone feel welcome, especially if they are new to a group. Not everyone finds it easy to make friends. Even if you don't want to be best friends with someone, there's no harm in being nice to them."

Helpful Addresses and Phone Numbers

Talking about problems can really help. If you can't talk to someone close to you, then try getting in touch with one of these organizations:

Just for Kids Hotline
Tel: 1-888-594-kids
A 24-hour free helpline for children. The number won't show up on a telephone bill.

National Youth Crisis Hotline
Tel: 800-442-HOPE (442-4673)
Provides services for children and youth who are depressed over family or school problems.
Operates 24 hours.

New York Society for the Prevention of Cruelty to Children
Tel: (212) 233-5500
www.nyspcc.org

Kids Help Phone, Canada
Tel: 1-800-668-6868
Toll Free anywhere in Canada.
English or French, 24 hours a day, 365 days a year.

Child Welfare League of America
Tel: (202) 638-2952
www.cwla.org
A confidential helpline offering advice for parents and children.

On the Web

These websites are also helpful. You can get in touch with some of them using email:

www.childhelpusa.org

www.girlsandboystown.org

www.kidshealth.org

www.shykids.com/

www.kidshelpphone.ca/en/

www.there4me.com

Further Reading

If you want to read more about loneliness and making friends, try:

Even Sharks Need Friends by Elaine Pease (peasepodbooks.com)

Talking About: Being An Immigrant by Sarah Levete (Stargazer Books)

Friends: Making Them & Keeping Them by Erin Falligant and Michelle Watkins (American Girl Library)

Making Friends by Fred Rogers (Paperstar)

How Kids Make Friends: Secrets for Making Lots of Friends, No Matter How Shy You Are by Lonny Michelle (Freedom Publishing Company)

Index

Photocredits

l-left, r-right, b-bottom, t-top, c-center, m-middle

All photos from istockphoto.com except: Cover tl, 15—Comstock.

Cover tc, 2—Brand X Pictures. 12—Select Photos/Marc Arundale.

19—Photodisc. 20, 28tr—TongRo Image Stock.

All the photos in this book have been posed by models.